AMERICAN
FOOTBALL

PLAY·THE·GAME

AMERICAN FOOTBALL

Colin Nelson ·

Ward Lock Limited · London

First published in Great Britain in 1988
by Ward Lock Limited, 8 Clifford Street
London W1X 1RB, an Egmont Company

Series Editor Ian Morrison
Designed by Anita Ruddell
Figure drawings by Jerry Malone
Diagrams by Peter Bull Art

Text set in Helvetica
by Hourds Typographica, Stafford, England
Printed and bound in Great Britain
by Richard Clay Ltd, Bungay, Suffolk

British Library Cataloguing in Publication Data
Nelson, Colin
  Play the game : American football.
  1. American football
  I. Title
  796.332

  ISBN 0-7063-6666-2

Acknowledgments

The author and publishers would like to
thank Colorsport for supplying the
photographs reproduced in this book.

Frontispiece: **Action from a game between
the Tampa Bay Bandits and the
Philadelphia Stars.**

CONTENTS

FOREWORD

American football is the fastest-growing participatory sport in the United Kingdom. It is being played in almost every major town and city throughout Britain and the growth of the game is accelerating all the time.

The NFL has discovered a new market on this side of the Atlantic. Marino, Elway and 'The Fridge' are names that are fast becoming as well known here as in America, and English fans have filled Wembley stadium to capacity the past two years watching the Bears, Giants, Broncos and the Rams in action.

The popularity of American football and the desire to play the game has led to the formation of over 200 senior and about 100 junior teams in British American football. With more and more youngsters in the UK becoming involved in the game, it's just a matter of time before more home-grown talent join British stars Vince Abbott of the San Diego Chargers, Mick Luckhurst of the Atlanta Falcons and John Smith, formerly of the New England Patriots, on NFL playing fields.

American football is also growing outside the UK. Though the game here is still developing, it is already well-established in

many European countries. Italy, Germany, France, Holland, Austria and Australia all have well-developed leagues (there are 300 teams in Germany and Italy alone!), and in Japan there are universities that have fielded American football teams for over ten years.

When it is played correctly, American football is a game that can be compared to chess. Both games require skill, tactics, precise moves and a respect for the opponent. But unlike chess, the game of American football is played by athletes who combine power with speed, finesse and agility. It requires a high degree of coaching in all aspects of the game; offensive, defensive, and special teams (field goals, punting, kick-offs). There are twenty-two positions on the offensive and defensive units, and each position requires its own level of skill and expertise. Both player and coach must be students of the game in order to excel. There is so much activity that occurs during each play that seven referees

are needed to oversee the play. On the surface, American football is a difficult game to understand – but it is an easy game to enjoy.

To best understand and play the game, years of experience are usually required. Each player on a team has different responsibilities – some players run with the ball, some throw it, some catch it, and some merely block the others. A truly successful team is a unit where all players play together towards a common goal – but don't be frustrated, even if you're not a member of a team you too can learn to become an expert on American football. To further the standards of British American Football, the sport needs well-informed students of the game. Although there is no substitute for individual coaching, this easy-to-read book, *Play the Game: American Football,* should give most fans or players all the help that they need to understand the basics of the game. Whether you're an 'armchair quarterback', a sports master, a player or just a complete rookie, *Play the Game: American Football* will make you more knowledgeable, and will increase your enjoyment of a most exciting game.

Lance L. Cone
Chairman of the British American Football Association

HISTORY & DEVELOPMENT OF AMERICAN FOOTBALL

Football was introduced to the United States by English settlers at the turn of the seventeenth century. The game, similar to the present-day game of soccer, was played with a round inflated ball. Two hundred years passed before this game was introduced into the American colleges and in 1867 the first rules of American football were drawn up.

Because they were formulated at Princeton College they became known as the Princeton rules, and were for a twenty-five-a-side version of Association football. About the same time, Rutgers also formulated rules of a similar game and on 6 November 1869 the two teams met at New Brunswick and played under Rutgers' rules, which were a modification of the rules of the London Football Association.

Rutgers' rules also stipulated twenty-five players per side, a pitch measuring 360ft (109·7m) by 225ft (68·6m) and with goals the same width as in soccer, at 24ft (7·3m). The first team scoring six goals were deemed the winners. The important difference between this and the Association game was that under Rutgers' rules the ball could be kicked, or 'batted' with the hand. Running with the ball or throwing it were, however, not allowed. Rutgers beat Princeton 6-4 in that historic first match.

When the two teams met a fortnight later the Princeton rules were used. The main difference between the two sets of rules allowed for a player making a clean catch under Princeton rules to have a free kick. Princeton gained revenge by winning 8-0 (the first to eight being the winner this time).

The game soon caught on in other colleges, notably at Columbia and Yale. Harvard revived football in 1871 and they played what was known as the 'Boston Game'. It was basically soccer but the ball (round) could be picked up and the player could run with it . . . a form of rugby if you like!

Harvard played the McGill University Football Club of Montreal twice in 1874. McGill played English rugby and Harvard were so impressed with this variation of football they discussed with Yale the possibility of drawing up a new set of rules along the lines of rugby. Princeton and Columbia were also invited to a meeting and in 1876 the Intercollegiate Football Association was formed and the English Rugby Union code of rules was adopted, but with some modifications.

In 1880, Walter Chauncey Camp of Yale changed the whole face of the game. He felt it needed to be more imaginative. He reduced the number of players from fifteen to eleven; he abolished the scrummage and introduced the scrimmage; and he established the team line-up that became standard . . . seven linemen, a quarterback, two halfbacks and a fullback. Two years later Camp introduced the downs and yardage rules. Originally it was 5 yards in three downs. As it became essential to know how far a player had advanced it was necessary to draw a series of parallel lines across the pitch at five-yard intervals, thus giving it a gridiron appearance. And so was born the word 'gridiron' into American football. The scoring system of different points for touchdowns, field goals, 'points after' touchdowns, and safeties was adopted in 1883 and five years later Camp got the rules changed to allow tackling of the player with the ball below the waist.

American football was well and truly born. All identity with soccer had certainly disappeared and the new game was far more strategic than rugby.

As the sport went into the 1890s it was apparent that it was becoming tough and dangerous. Coaches were employing strong-arm tactics to stop opposing players, although they were within the laws. In 1894 representatives of the leading college teams met, and certain mass plays, which resulted

in batteries of men taking opposing players out of the game, were outlawed. At the same meeting the playing time was cut from ninety to seventy minutes.

Teams still continued to play with brutal tactics and devised new types of plays. Pennsylvania, for example, won sixty-five of the sixty-six games played between 1894 and 1898 with their 'guards back' attack. Despite changes in the rules over the years the roughness continued and in 1905 there were eighteen deaths in American football games throughout the United States. The country was outraged and President Roosevelt himself called representatives of Yale, Harvard and Princeton together and told them the brutality and foul play within the sport had to stop.

More than sixty representatives from college teams met in December 1905 to iron out the problems. Captain Pierce of West Point sat at the head of the meeting, and the Intercollegiate Association of the United States was formed. (It became the National Collegiate Athletic Association (NCAA), in 1910.) The following year it made major changes to the rules: playing time was cut to sixty minutes; the forward pass was legalized; a neutral zone between the two

lines of scrimmage was established; the yards to gain was increased to ten. But the biggest problem, interlocked interference, continued and the game remained hazardous.

In 1910 however, interlocked interference was banned, along with pushing and pulling of the ball carrier. The game became a lot safer but had, as a result, become more defensive. To ease that problem the 10 yards gain rule was increased from three to four downs in 1912. The length of the field was also reduced to 100yd (91·4m) and end zones were added. The limit on the distance a ball could be thrown forward was also lifted (it was previously 20yd (18·29m), and the touchdown value was increased from five to six. There have been few changes since then.

Offense and defense formations are the key part of a successful American football team and in the late 1930s George Halas of the Chicago Bears, together with the University of Chicago coach, Clark Shaughnessy, developed the famous T-formation which now forms the basis of all modern-day offenses.

In 1945, Michigan started using whole platoons of men for offensive and defensive lines but this was outlawed in 1953, when only one player at a time was allowed to be substituted. However, in 1965 wholesale substitutions were permitted and all teams now have batteries of men to fulfil each specific role.

The professional game is tremendously popular on both sides of the Atlantic and is the national winter sport in the United States. But college football remains very popular and it is to the colleges each year that professional teams turn to strengthen their squads. A selection made right at the end of the football season by professional teams of all eligible college players, known as the

The quarterback about to pass in a game between the New York Giants and the St Louis Cardinals.

AMERICAN · FOOTBALL

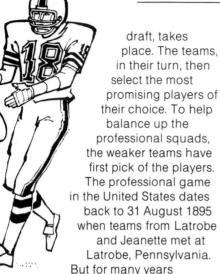

draft, takes place. The teams, in their turn, then select the most promising players of their choice. To help balance up the professional squads, the weaker teams have first pick of the players. The professional game in the United States dates back to 31 August 1895 when teams from Latrobe and Jeanette met at Latrobe, Pennsylvania. But for many years the professional game was overshadowed by the college game. At the turn of the century leading college players joined professional teams because it gave them a chance to continue playing after their college careers ended. They did not join teams for the financial rewards, which were nowhere near as great as those of today.

It was not until 1920 that the American Professional Football Association (APFA) was formed at Canton with Tom Thorpe as its first president. After a disastrous inaugural year it was restructured in 1921 with a new president, Joseph Carr of Columbus, Ohio. Franchises cost as little as fifty dollars at that time . . . today you are talking in terms of millions of dollars. The APFA changed its name to the National Football League (NFL) in 1922.

The first league season was in 1921 when thirteen teams took part, with the Chicago Staleys emerging as the inaugural champions. If you look at the names of the other twelve teams you will see little resemblance to the NFL teams of today. The other twelve were: Buffalo All-Americans, Akron Pros, Green Bay Packers, Canton Bulldogs, Dayton Triangles, Rock Island Independents, Chicago Cardinals, Cleveland Indians, Rochester Jeffersons, Detroit Heralds, Columbus Panhandles, and Cincinatti Celts.

The professional game received its biggest boost in 1925 when Harold 'Red' Grange of Illinois turned professional with the Chicago Bears. He was the most outstanding college player at the time and the publicity his move attracted sent attendance figures soaring. In his first two months touring with the Bears he pulled in such vast crowds that he pocketed $250,000. Despite Grange's appeal the professional game was, as a whole, attracting average crowds of around only twenty thousand while top college games were attracting regular fifty thousand crowds, and in some cases attendance figures went into six figures.

In 1933 the NFL was split into two leagues, the Eastern and Western Divisions, with the two winners meeting at the end of the season for the World Championship. The Chicago Bears beat the New York Giants 23-21 to claim the title as the first world champions of American football.

By 1946 the professional game had captured people's imagination and the attendance at the New York Polo Grounds for the World Championship between the Giants and Bears attracted a crowd of 58,346. The professional game had arrived, and was here to stay.

The success of the professional game led to the formation of a second league in 1946 with the inauguration of the All American Conference. The two leagues were forced to merge at the end of 1949 and for the next three seasons the two leagues were known as the American and National Conferences. They became the Eastern and Western Conferences in 1953 and in 1960 another new league was formed, the American Football League, with eight teams. The NFL was extended to thirteen teams that same year and the two leagues each had two divisions/conferences. The winners of each division/conference met to decide the champions of the AFL and the NFL but the two champions did *not* meet to find the ultimate champions.

That situation was, however, rectified at the end of the 1966 season when the AFL champions played the NFL champions for the sport's most cherished prize, the Super Bowl. Green Bay from the NFL beat Kansas City from the AFL 35-10 to win the first ever Super Bowl.

Today, twenty-eight teams make up the National Football League with fourteen in the American Football Conference (AFC) and fourteen in the National Football Conference (NFC). Each conference is split into three divisions known as the Eastern, Central and Western Divisions. At the end of the season the top five teams in each Conference play off to find the conference winners and the AFC and NFC champions meet in the Super Bowl.

Television coverage in Great Britain since 1982 has made Sunday night (and now Tuesday as well) compulsive viewing for the British fans of the sport, and names like Dan Marino, Jim McMahon and William 'The Refrigerator' Perry are as much household names as their British soccer counterparts Ian Rush, Glenn Hoddle and Bryan Robson.

It may come as a surprise to learn that the first American football game to be played in Britain was as long ago as 1910 when teams from two American warships met each other in front of a crowd of four thousand at Northfleet in Kent. But the sport never really caught on until the public's imagination was captured following Channel 4's coverage of the sport. In the London, Birmingham and Manchester areas, groups of enthusiasts got together to form teams, The leading British team is the London Ravens and they have dominated the game since their formation. The first organized British leagues were formed in March 1984 when the nineteen-team American Football League of the United Kingdom (AFL) and the seven-team British American Football Federation (BAFF) were formed. Teams suddenly sprung up at an alarming rate, but problems arose. There were plenty of people interested in playing but clubs needed officials and of course,

there was the age-old problem of . . . money. It is quite expensive to equip an American football squad.

Another league, the United Kingdom American Football Association, was subsequently started, as was the Budweiser League. The latter has since had the biggest influence on the British game because of its sponsorship from brewers Watney Mann. The new league's arrival led to the ultimate demise of the BAFL at the end of 1986.

Proof, at last, that the game is being well organized in Britain is apparent when you look at the attendance for the 1987 Budweiser Bowl between the London Ravens and the Manchester All-Stars. The Ravens won the title in front of a crowd of thirteen thousand at Loftus Road, home of Queen's Park Rangers FC.

West Germany, Finland and Italy are all strongholds of the game in Europe. The first Italian team, the Milan Rhinos, was formed in 1976 and in Finland the first team was formed in 1979. Today there are thirty-two teams in eighteen Finnish cities. The sport became organized in Germany in 1980, the year after the formation of the country's first team, the Dusseldorf Panthers. There are currently about fifty teams in the German League.

The European Football League was formed in 1985 and has forty-five thousand players; six hundred men's teams, one hundred junior teams, and eight women's teams. The stature of the game in Europe is confirmed by the fact that Matti Lindholm, a linebacker with the Helsinki Giants, was invited to attend the Minnesota Vikings 1987 summer training camp.

American football is exciting to watch; it is exciting to play, it looks complicated when you first see it, but it is basically a simple game with simple rules. The tactics of the offense and defense are what give it that special fascination. It is easy to see why more than three million British fans sit glued to their television sets on Sunday and Tuesday evenings.

EQUIPMENT & TERMINOLOGY

The pitch

All pitches have standard measurements, unlike their Association Football counterparts. The playing area of the American football pitch is 300ft (91·4m) long by 160ft (48·77m) wide. Across the width of the pitch are parallel lines at 5yd (4·57m) intervals. These markings give the pitch the 'gridiron' effect. Each of the 5-yard lines has two lines marked at right angles to it and at a position 70ft 9in (21·56m) from each sideline. Known as hashmarks, these indicate the central playing strips. All plays must start between the two markers on or between the appropriate 5-yard line. It makes no difference where play comes to a halt, the ball will always be re-sited between these lines. Most pitches, particularly in the NFL, also have interim markings at 1yd (0·91m) intervals, to provide an accurate placement of the ball at the commencement of all downs.

At each end of the playing area are two further areas which are the width of the pitch and 10yd (9·14m) deep. These are the end zones, which are the scoring areas for touchdowns. On the back lines of the end zones are positioned the goal posts. In the professional game they are shaped like a 'T' with the support of the posts behind the line

but with the cross bar level with the end line. The goals are 18ft 6in (5·64m) wide and the crossbar is at a point 10ft (3·05m) above the ground. The tops of the posts extend to approximately 30ft (9·14m) from the ground.

A line called the 2-yard line is marked on the pitch at a point 12yd (10·97m) from the end line and centred between the goalposts. Unlike rugby, the kick is not taken level with

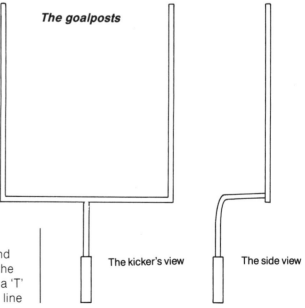

The goalposts

The kicker's view   The side view

The pitch

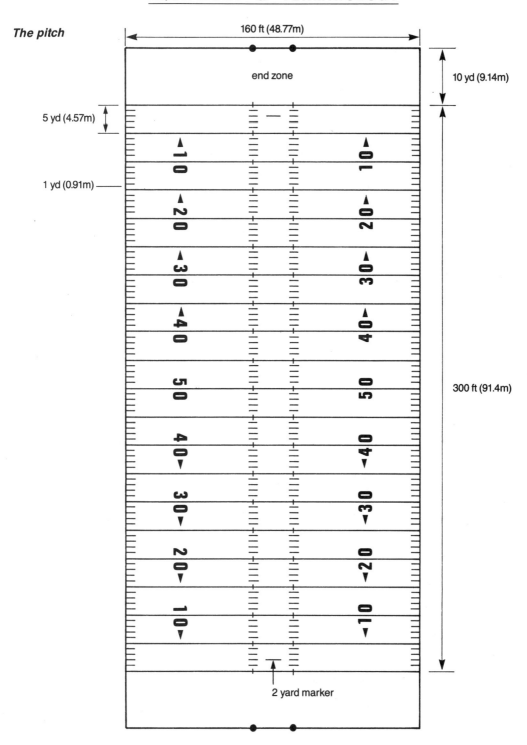

160 ft (48.77m)

end zone

10 yd (9.14m)

5 yd (4.57m)

1 yd (0.91m)

300 ft (91.4m)

2 yard marker

The ball

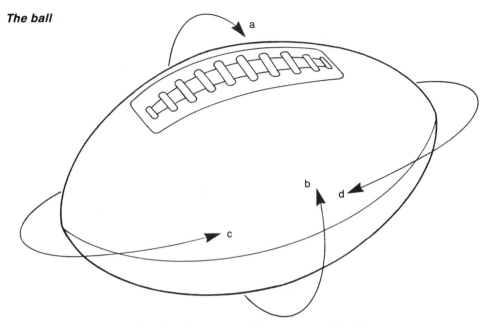

The circumference around the narrow part of the ball (a-b) is approx. 21½ in (54.61 cm) and around the 'long part' (c-d) is approx. 28½ in (72.39 cm)

the point of the touchdown, but from the 2-yard line.

The playing surface can be either grass or an artificial material. Both are popular in the professional game although teams are tending to revert to conventional grass surfaces because of the increasing number of injuries on the artificial ones in recent years.

The ball

The ball is oval-shaped and pointed at each end (similar to a rugby ball). It should weigh approximately 14oz (397g) and should be about 11–11¼in (27·9–28·6cm) long. The circumference around the centre of the ball (the 'wide' part) is approximately 21½in (54·6cm) and the circumference around the 'long' part is approximately 28½in (72·4cm). The majority of the balls used are made out of pebbled leather, but some are also made out of pigskin.

Player's equipment

American football is a tough game and all players need protection. If you took a player's outer clothing off him you would see that virtually every part of his body is protected.

Let's see what the average player wears for protection, starting from the top and working down . . .

The helmet with built-in face mask and chin strap reduces the risk of facial injury and in particular damage to the nose and mouth.

Shoulder pads reduce the possibility of dislocated shoulders, for so long the curse of rugby players, many of whom have now also taken to wearing them.

Elbow pads are often used when playing on artificial surfaces.

Gloves are optional and the type worn is down to personal preference. Most players do not wear gloves and have tape wrapped around their fingers to help them when catching the ball.

Hip pads give protection to the hips, waist, and groin.

Thigh pads help protect the thigh muscles.

Knee pads are, like elbow pads, quite useful when playing on artificial surfaces.

Shoes are similar to football boots. For grass surfaces the moulded rubber or plastic-studded boots are worn. When playing on an artificial surface the rubberized sole type are preferred.
An aid to kickers is the **kicking tee**, a small plastic device used to hold the ball in position at the kick-off.

All players from the same team wear an identical outfit over that lot and each player is numbered. Because players all have specific roles on the field, squad members are numbered in accordance with their role so as to help the officials. Each of the officials also have a number on their backs for identification purposes. This is how players are numbered:

1–19 quarterbacks and kickers
20–49 running backs and defensive backs
50–59 centers and linebackers
60–79 defensive linemen and interior offensive linemen (including centers)
80–89 wide receivers and tight ends
90–99 further defensive linemen and linebackers

So much for the playing area, the ball, protective clothing and the equipment; now for a new experience: American football terminology. When you look at, for example, rugby, which, after all, is not dissimilar to the gridiron game, its terminology pales into insignificance in comparison. Just look at this . . .

TERMINOLOGY

Audible   The audible is the signal(s) called by the quarterback at the scrimmage line which will tell his team-mates what play they will use when on the offense.

Back   The name given to players behind the line of scrimmage. On the offensive team the back is allowed to carry the ball.

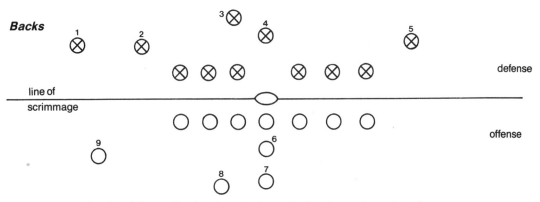

On the defense, linebackers 1–5 are the backs, and on the offense, players 6–9 are the backs. No 6 is the quarterback, 7 and 8 are the running backs and no 9 the wide receiver.

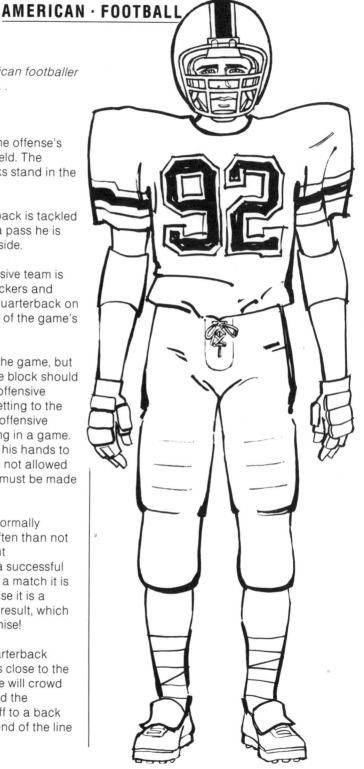

Equipment

This is what the average American footballer looks like on the outside, but . . .

Backfield   The area behind the offense's line of scrimmage is the backfield. The quarterback and running backs stand in the backfield.

Blindside   When the quarterback is tackled from behind while attempting a pass he is said to be tackled on the blindside.

Blitz   A blitz is when the offensive team is rushed by the defensive linebackers and safeties in order to tackle the quarterback on a passing play. The blitz is one of the game's most spectacular sights.

Blocking   Blocking is part of the game, but the rules dictate strictly how the block should be made. Blocks are made by offensive players to stop an opponent getting to the man with the ball. You will see offensive linemen doing the most blocking in a game. A blocker is not allowed to use his hands to grab or hold a player and he is not allowed to tackle or trip him. All blocks must be made from in front of the player.

Bomb   A long pass which is normally thrown as a last resort. More often than not it will fail to produce a result but occasionally it turns out to be a successful pass. In the closing seconds of a match it is often called a Hail Mary, because it is a last-ditched effort to salvage a result, which is more of a prayer than a promise!

Bootleg   Often called the 'quarterback keeper', it is when the offense is close to the defense's goal line. The defense will crowd the centre of the scrimmage and the quarterback will fake a hand-off to a back and make the run around the end of the line and go for the touchdown.

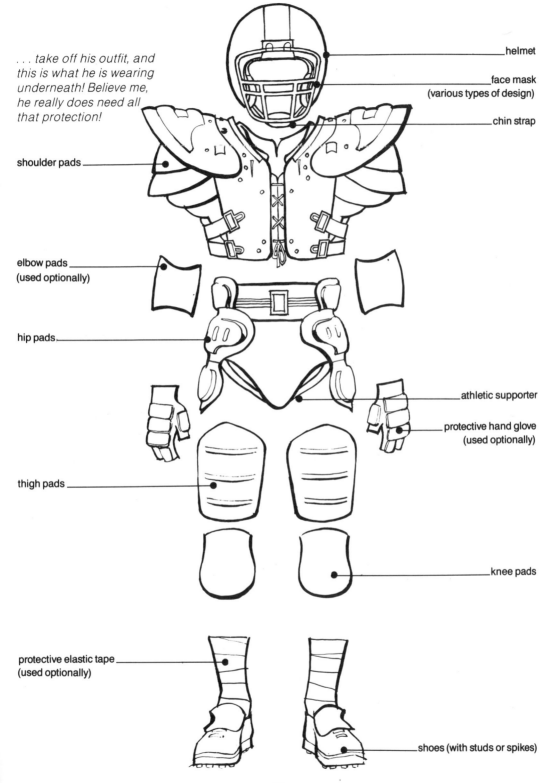

. . . take off his outfit, and this is what he is wearing underneath! Believe me, he really does need all that protection!

helmet

face mask
(various types of design)

chin strap

shoulder pads

elbow pads
(used optionally)

hip pads

athletic supporter

protective hand glove
(used optionally)

thigh pads

knee pads

protective elastic tape
(used optionally)

shoes (with studs or spikes)

Blocking

Center   The center is positioned in the middle of the line of scrimmage. He snaps the ball back to the quarterback.

Chain gang (or chain crew)   They are the three officials on the sideline who measure the yards gained or lost by the offensive team, and indicate the number of downs. The figure displayed indicates the next down.

Coffin corner   The part of the playing area on the 1-yard line where the sideline and goal line meets. There are four coffin corners

on a pitch and from a kick-off it is a useful place to try and land the kick.

Completion   A successfully caught pass is a completion.

Coverage   An expression to describe the type of marking. One offensive player may be marked by two defensive players. He is said to have double coverage.

Cut   When a ball carrier is running at speed and suddenly changes direction he is said to have made a cut.

line of scrimmage

The center

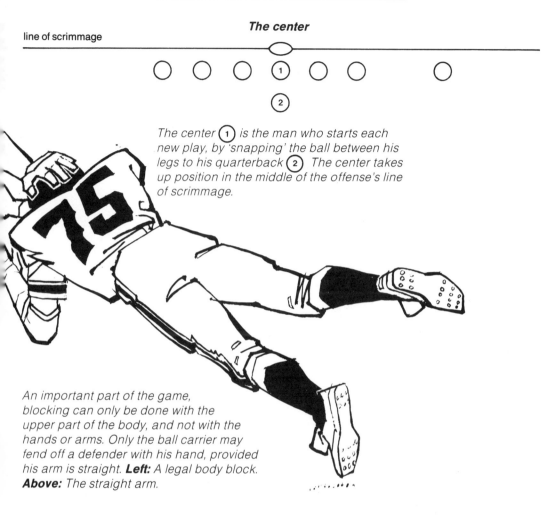

The center ① is the man who starts each new play, by 'snapping' the ball between his legs to his quarterback ② The center takes up position in the middle of the offense's line of scrimmage.

An important part of the game, blocking can only be done with the upper part of the body, and not with the hands or arms. Only the ball carrier may fend off a defender with his hand, provided his arm is straight. **Left:** A legal body block. **Above:** The straight arm.

Dead ball Any ball that is out of play is dead. A ball also becomes dead when the referee blows his whistle or when the clock is stopped.

Defense The team that does not have the ball is the defense. However, once the defense regains possession of the ball it automatically becomes the offense, and the same applies in reverse.

Defensive backs The safeties and cornerbacks of the defensive side make up the defensive backs.

Delay Once a play has come to an end the next play must start within thirty seconds. If it doesn't there is said to be a delay and the offensive team is penalized five yards.

Direct snap As opposed to the normal snap, when the center 'snaps' the ball back to his quarterback immediately behind him, the direct snap is when the receiving player is standing approximately seven yards (6·4m) behind him. If the center 'snapped' a ball back to a punter or kicker for an extra point or field goal it would then be described as a direct snap.

Defensive backs

In this defensive line-up players 1–4 are the defensive backs. 1 and 4 are cornerbacks, 2 and 3 are safeties.

Down   The offensive team has four attempts, using a series of plays, to gain 10yd (9·14m). Each of those attempts is called a down.

Draw play   Often used to foil a blitz, the quarterback will step back as if to throw the ball but, on seeing an opening, will give the ball to a running back who will head for the opening in an effort to score the touchdown, or gain further yards.

Dropback   When the quarterback steps backwards ready to make a pass, he drops back; also known as a fadeback.

Encroachment   If a player leaves the line of scrimmage and makes contact with an opposing player before the ball has been snapped it is an encroachment.

End line   The two extreme ends of the playing area are the end lines. If the ball goes beyond an end line it is dead.

End zone   The areas at each end of the field; they are 160ft (48·77m) wide and 10yd (9·14m) deep. It is to this designated area that the ball must travel before a touchdown can be scored.

Extra point   After a touchdown the successful team is allowed the chance of an extra point by kicking the ball over the crossbar from the 2-yard line. It is similar to the conversion in rugby except that the kicker does not have a direct attempt at the goal. The ball has to be snapped back by the centre and then positioned on the ground for the kicker to make his attempt. The defensive line make a rush for him in an effort to prevent the successful kick.

Facemasking   One of the sport's most dangerous acts, it is when a defensive player tackles a runner by his mask. Officials keep a careful watch to make sure facemasking does not take place.

Fadeback   see Dropback.

Fair catch   When a player catches a kicked ball he can either carry on running upfield or he can indicate a fair catch by raising his arm while the ball is still in flight. This means that when he catches the ball he will not be interfered with by the defensive team. He must, however, once he has made the catch, not advance further upfield. His team's offensive drive will start from the point where the catch is made. (But between the hashmarks.)

Fake   When a quarterback gives a 'dummy' to the defensive team he is said to have made a fake. It often takes the form of a

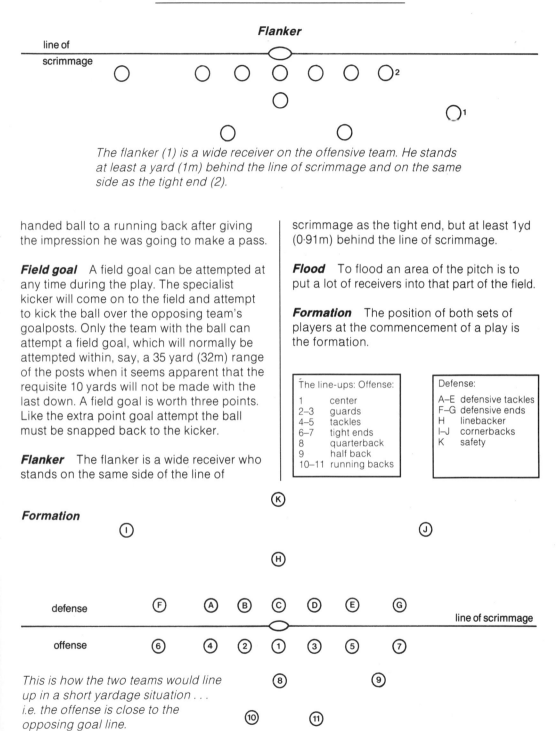

Flanker

line of scrimmage

The flanker (1) is a wide receiver on the offensive team. He stands at least a yard (1m) behind the line of scrimmage and on the same side as the tight end (2).

handed ball to a running back after giving the impression he was going to make a pass.

Field goal   A field goal can be attempted at any time during the play. The specialist kicker will come on to the field and attempt to kick the ball over the opposing team's goalposts. Only the team with the ball can attempt a field goal, which will normally be attempted within, say, a 35 yard (32m) range of the posts when it seems apparent that the requisite 10 yards will not be made with the last down. A field goal is worth three points. Like the extra point goal attempt the ball must be snapped back to the kicker.

Flanker   The flanker is a wide receiver who stands on the same side of the line of

scrimmage as the tight end, but at least 1yd (0·91m) behind the line of scrimmage.

Flood   To flood an area of the pitch is to put a lot of receivers into that part of the field.

Formation   The position of both sets of players at the commencement of a play is the formation.

The line-ups: Offense:		Defense:
1	center	A–E defensive tackles
2–3	guards	F–G defensive ends
4–5	tackles	H linebacker
6–7	tight ends	I–J cornerbacks
8	quarterback	K safety
9	half back	
10–11	running backs	

Formation

defense

line of scrimmage

offense

This is how the two teams would line up in a short yardage situation . . . i.e. the offense is close to the opposing goal line.

Fumble   A player fumbles if he drops the ball while carrying it and it stays in play. If a player fumbles, the ball can be collected by a player from either side.

Game plan   Before each game the coach will have a strategic plan worked out for every type of play.

Goal line   The goal line is situated parallel with and 10yd (9·14m) from the end line. It indicates the end of the playing area and the start of the end zone.

Hail Mary   A 'bomb' played in the closing seconds of a match.

Hand-off   Used in offensive play when one player hands the ball to another, as opposed to passing it. Hand-offs often confuse the defense.

Hang time   The amount of time a punted ball is in the air is referred to as the hang time.

Hashmarks   The hashmarks indicate the central playing strip between which all new plays start.

Hole   When an offensive lineman creates a gap for a runner to run through he is said to have created a hole.

Huddle   You will see both sets of players getting together in between plays to discuss the next strategy. This is called the huddle.

Incompletion   A pass that is neither intercepted nor caught is an incompletion.

Ineligible receiver   An offensive player who is not permitted to act as a receiver, is an ineligible receiver. Tackles, guards and centers are usually ineligible receivers.

Opposing linemen at the line of scrimmage.

Interior linemen

line of

scrimmage

The five men in the middle of the offense's line of scrimmage are the interior linemen, and they are: (1) center; (2) and (3) guards; (4) and (5) tackles.

Interception   When a defensive player catches a pass from an offensive player he has made an interception. He then becomes an offensive player and will attempt to make as much ground as he can upfield, before his team's special offensive unit comes on to the field of play.

Intentional grounding   To avoid being sacked the quarterback may deliberately throw an incompletion so as not to lose any yards. This is intentional grounding and is illegal.

Interior linemen   The five players who form the inside of the offensive line are the interior linemen. They consist of the center, two tackles and two guards.

Kick-off return   The number of yards gained by the man making the catch from the kick-off.

Lateral   A pass that travels either behind, or along the line of scrimmage is called a lateral.

Lineman   Any player that stands on the line of scrimmage is a lineman.

Line of scrimmage   It is an imaginary line drawn across the field where the last play ended. The next play begins from along that line and at a point between the two hashmarks. The opposing linemen face each other at the line, awaiting the commencement of the next play.

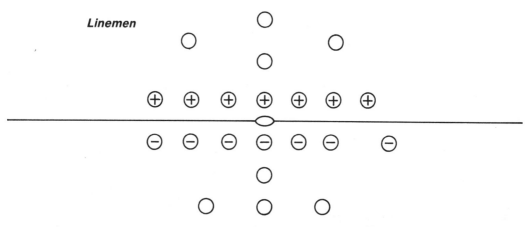

Linemen

All players who line up along the line of scrimmage are linemen. In this diagram all players marked ⊖ are offensive linemen and players marked ⊕ are defensive linemen.

EQUIPMENT · & · TERMINOLOGY

Man-to-man   As its name implies, this is when a pass receiver is marked closely, normally by a defensive linebacker, cornerback or safety.

Neutral zone   At the line of scrimmage the area between the ball and each set of linemen is called the neutral zone.

Offense   The team in possession of the ball is the offense.

Offside   A player is offside if any part of his body is beyond the line of scrimmage at the moment the ball is snapped.

Onside kick   A short kick from the kick-off is an onside kick. It must travel the minimum distance of 10yd (9·14m) but if successful, the team kicking off has a chance of regaining possession of the ball.

Out-of-bounds   The areas outside the sidelines and end lines are out-of-bounds. The lines themselves also form part of the out-of-bounds area so, any player or ball on or beyond them is out-of-bounds.

Overtime   Overtime is the equivalent to soccer's extra time and is used when the scores are level at the end of the four quarters. Once a team scores in an overtime period that is the end of the match.

Pass interference   If a player deliberately prevents an opponent from catching the ball it is a pass interference and the guilty player is penalized.

Penalty   The number of penalty offences in American football are numerous. The price you pay for a penalty is the loss of yardage, the loss of downs or, in some cases, both, depending upon the seriousness of the foul. For a list of offences and their penalties see pages 48 and 49.

Penalty marker   If an official spots an infringement of the rules, he throws a yellow weighted duster to the ground.

Offside
Any player who advances beyond the line of scrimmage before the snap is offside. The penalty is 5 yards.

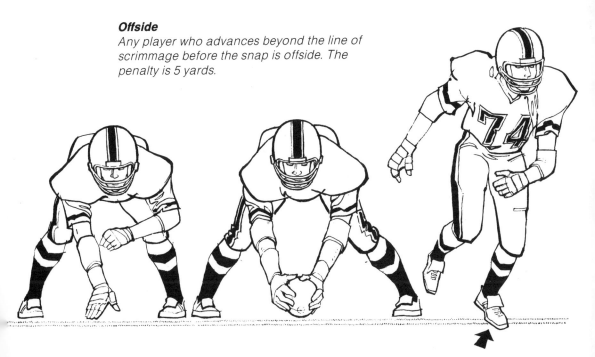

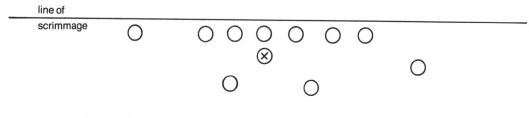

The pocket

After taking the ball from the snap, the quarterback ⊗ will step back ready to make a pass and his linemen and running backs will form a 'pocket' around him in order to give him protection.

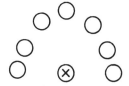

Personal foul When a passer or kicker is hit, punched, kneed, piled-on or clipped it is a personal foul.

Pitchout It sounds more like a baseball term but it is not . . . it is when the quarterback pitches the ball underarm to a running back rather than handing it to him.

Play action When a quarterback fakes a handout to a running back he keeps the ball and then makes a pass.

Pocket To give the quarterback space to make a pass, his linemen, and often his running backs as well, will create a pocket for him from which to throw.

Possession A player is in possession of the ball if he has taken control of the ball cleanly and is in a position to effect another move in conjunction with the rules.

Post pattern When a wide receiver runs down the sidelines and then sharply cuts infield to receive his pass.

Punt If a team is on their fourth down and unlikely to make their 10 yards the kicker will punt the ball as far upfield as he can. Consequently, after giving the other side possession, this will have forced them deep into their own territory. To make a punt the ball is snapped to the kicker from the scrimmage. He then quickly drops the ball and kicks it before it hits the ground.

Punt return The distance the player who catches a punt advances upfield is called the punt return.

Quarter A game consists of four quarters, each of fifteen minutes duration. Overtime is played if the teams are level at the end of four quarters.

Post pattern

In the post pattern the receiver will make his run, pursued by a defender, and will then suddenly cut infield to collect a ball thrown by his quarterback to a pre-determined part of the field.

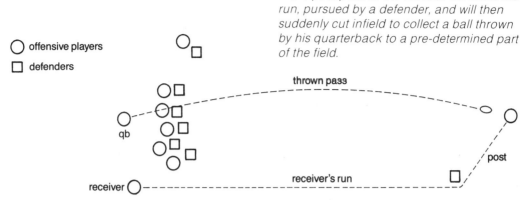

Quarterback sneak   When the quarterback attempts to rush through the line of scrimmage on his own rather than passing it is a quarterback sneak . . . what else could it be called!

Quick count   Calling of numbers by the quarterback to his team mates is all important at the line of scrimmage. Quick-acting defensive players will pick up such calls. To confuse the defense the numbers are often abbreviated by the quarterback. This is known as the quick count.

Recover   When a player regains possession of the ball after a fumble he makes a recover.

Return   The amount of ground made in yards by a player who collects a kick or intercepts a pass.

Reverse   A quick-action play designed to confuse the defensive team. The quarterback will hand-off to a running back who runs one way across the line of scrimmage but will then hand-off to another running back going the other way. It is a very effective way of side-stepping the defense, and a very popular play.

Running play   A play from the line of scrimmage where no pass is made.

Rushing play   Any play that involves running with the ball after a hand-off, a lateral pass, or a pitchout is a rushing play.

Sack   When the quarterback is tackled in his own backfield while in possession of the ball he is said to have been sacked. Such a tackle results in the offensive team losing yards because the quarterback is behind the line of scrimmage at the time of the sack. It is one of American football's great sights and defensive players who sack a quarterback get as much enjoyment as any player making a touchdown.

Safety   If an offensive player takes the ball on to, or over, his own goal line it is a safety and worth two points to the opposing side. This term also applies to the players who make up the last line of the defense.

Scrambling   When defenders break through the offensive line the quarterback has to scramble to avoid them.

Screen pass   A screen pass is when a hand-off to a running back is faked but a pass is made to another player behind the line of scrimmage. It is often used when the defensive team are planning a blitz.

Scrimmage A scrimmage starts when the ball is snapped back by the center and ends when the ball becomes dead.

Secondary The secondary is the defensive unit consisting of the cornerbacks and safeties. Their job is to prevent a pass.

Shift The shift is when offensive players swap positions before the snap to confuse the defensive linemen facing them.

Short yardage situation When the offense is close to the defense's goal line.

Sideline The two lines running the length of the field are the sidelines. If the ball goes over those lines, or is carried over by a player, the ball is dead.

Snap The action of the center, who passes the ball backwards through his legs to his quarterback.

*The snap
(side view).*

Discussing offensive strategy at the 'huddle'. It is the quarterback who calls the plays and who thus has the greatest influence on the course of a game.

Spearing

The dangerous act of throwing oneself headfirst at an opposing player is known as 'spearing'.

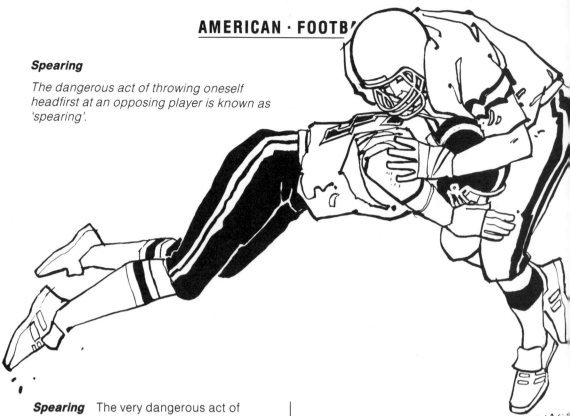

Spearing   The very dangerous act of diving, helmet first, at a player.

Spot pass   An act between the quarterback and his receiver whereby he will throw a pass to a predetermined part of the field. It is then the receiver's responsibility to get there!

Squib kick   A kick-off that rolls along the ground, bouncing irregularly as it goes.

Suicide squad   The name given to the special unit brought on for a kick-off. Their job is to make sure the receiver at the kick-off does not get the chance to progress up field too far.

Sweep   A running play whereby the running back takes the ball from his quarterback and sweeps round the line of scrimmage before making his run.

Tackling   The difference between tackling and blocking is that only the player with the ball can be *tackled*.

Time out   A stoppage in play during which the timekeeper will stop the clock. Each team is allowed three time outs per half.

Touchback   If a kick or punt forces the ball to go out of play over the defense's goal line it is a touchback and the defense restart play from their own 20-yard line.

Touchdown   Worth six points, a touchdown is scored when a player crosses the opposite goal line with the ball (he does not have to ground it) or takes a catch in the end zone.

Turnover   Losing the ball to the opposing side by fumbling or as the result of an interception is known as a turnover.

Two minute warning   In the final two minutes of each half the official will call a time out and advise both coaches that two minutes remain.

Tackling

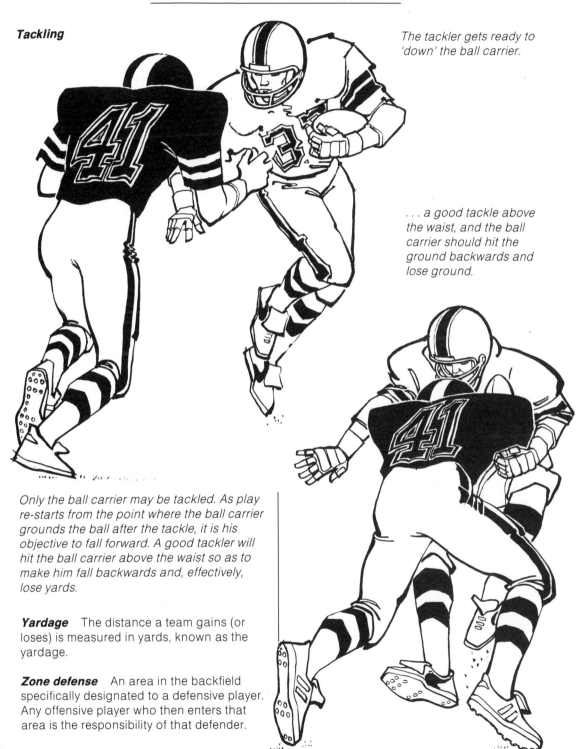

The tackler gets ready to 'down' the ball carrier.

. . . a good tackle above the waist, and the ball carrier should hit the ground backwards and lose ground.

Only the ball carrier may be tackled. As play re-starts from the point where the ball carrier grounds the ball after the tackle, it is his objective to fall forward. A good tackler will hit the ball carrier above the waist so as to make him fall backwards and, effectively, lose yards.

Yardage   The distance a team gains (or loses) is measured in yards, known as the yardage.

Zone defense   An area in the backfield specifically designated to a defensive player. Any offensive player who then enters that area is the responsibility of that defender.

THE GAME — A GUIDE

TEAMS · & · OFFICIALS

American football is played by two teams, each having eleven players on the field at one time. At all times one team is the attacking team (the offense) and the other the defending team (the defense). The offense is the team in possession of the ball.

Most professional clubs, however, have squads of forty-five players. Each squad consists of three teams: an offensive team, a defensive team and a special team. In addition they will have some reserves.

The game is controlled by seven officials who all carry a yellow weighted duster which is thrown to the ground when a foul is spotted. The senior official is the referee who always indicates a call. In the NFL the referee is distinguishable from his colleagues in that he wears a black cap as opposed to the white worn by the other officials. To assist the referee in making a decision on whether the offensive team have gained their required ten yards he is helped by the three-men chain gang, who measure distances and keep count of the downs.

Offense

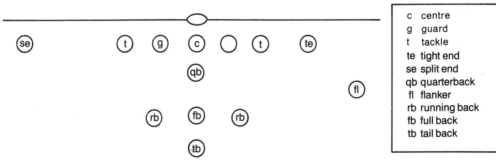

c	centre
g	guard
t	tackle
te	tight end
se	split end
qb	quarterback
fl	flanker
rb	running back
fb	full back
tb	tail back

The offensive positions are as follows:
There are thirteen players in the diagram but, of course, only eleven may be used at any one time. The full back and tail back are often used in place of the running backs.

Defense

A defensive formation showing all playing positions, including the little-used free safety.

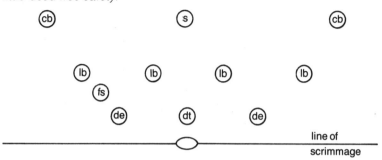

cb cornerback
s safety
lb linebacker
fs free safety
de defensive end
dt defensive tackle

Officials' positions

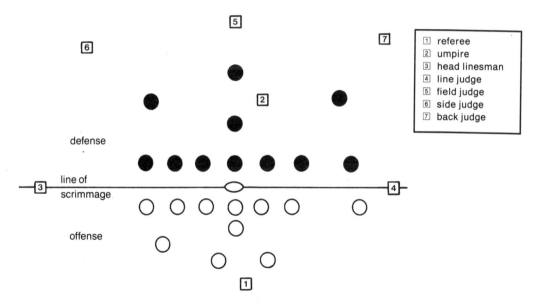

1 referee
2 umpire
3 head linesman
4 line judge
5 field judge
6 side judge
7 back judge

The teams

The offense   The eleven players on the offense are made up of a center, two guards, two tackles and two ends (either a tight end or split end depending on the play). These players form the offensive line and are then supplemented by a quarterback and running backs.

The defense   The make-up of the defensive unit obviously depends on the offensive line-up, but will generally consist of a nose guard, two tackles and linebackers (either the outside, inside or middle variety). The remaining players, usually four, are called the secondary or defensive backs and they can be either safeties or cornerbacks.

Special teams The remainder of the squad consists mostly of special teams. These units are used for a specific function, such as kick-offs, punts and field goals for the offense, and kick-off returns and punt returns for the defense.

American football embodies all of what sport is about – strength, speed, agility and organization, with one team trying to out-think and overpower the other in their quest to score points.

The officials

Seven officials control a professional game of American football. Because there is so much action in every play they are all fully utilized and keep a strict control of the game. The **referee** has overall control of the other officials. He positions himself behind the offensive team and is responsible for making all calls, even though it might have been another official who spotted an infringement. The **umpire** takes up his position behind the defensive backfield and he makes sure no infringements take place in that department. He also has the responsibility of recording time outs.

There are two officials on the line of scrimmage, one at each end. The **head lineman**, apart from looking for offsides and plays on his side of the line, is responsible for making sure the chain gang carry out their duties correctly. The official on the other end of the scrimmage line is the **line judge** who also looks out for offsides, encroachments, and all plays in his part of the field. He is also responsible for the timing of the game.

The other three officials all position themselves at the back of the defense. The **field judge** is positioned deep in the defense and his prime duty is to check the validity of

Fake or play? The quarterback presents the ball to one of his running backs.

REFEREE'S · SIGNALS

Offside or encroachment.

Illegal procedure.

Illegal motion.

Clipping.

Illegal use of the hands.

Intentional grounding.

Illegal forward pass.

Interference with a forward pass or fair catch.

Ineligible receiver downfield.

Ball caught out of bounds.

Time out lasted too long, or game delayed by offensive side.

A score.

Facemasking.

Illegal contact.

Illegally helping
the ball carrier.

Loss of down.

Invalid fair
catch signal.

Dead ball.

1st and 10.

Time out.

Blocking below the waist.

Unsportsmanlike conduct.

Roughing
the kicker.

Personal foul.

passes and punt catches. He also decides whether field goal attempts are good. The **side judge** lines up on the same side as the head lineman and keeps a watch on the wide receiver and running back on his side of the field. The **back judge** does the same, but on the opposite side of the field. He assists the field judge in deciding if a field goal attempt is successful.

The referee has a vast repertoire of signals he makes to the scorers, teams and fans to indicate what has happened. At senior level each referee also has a microphone connected to the public address system through which, in conjunction with his signals, he announces his decision and the proposed penalty.

PLAYING · THE · GAME

How to score points and their values

The object of the game is to score more points than your opponents. Points can be scored in different ways: the most valuable is a touchdown which is worth six points. A touchdown is scored by a team getting the ball into the opponents' end zone whilst keeping possession. This is achieved by a player holding the ball and running into the end zone or by a receiver catching a pass delivered into the same area. Unlike rugby, the ball does not have to be grounded for the touchdown.

A touchdown is immediately followed by the conversion which, if successful, is worth one further point. This is often referred to as the 'point after'. For the 'point after' the ball is placed on the 2-yard line from where it is 'snapped' to the kicker to despatch between the uprights and over the crossbar.

Following in value after a touchdown is a field goal worth three points. The field goal is kicked from about ten yards behind the scrimmage line to give the kicker more time, and protection from marauding defensive linemen. As the kick is from ten yards behind

the scrimmage, the kicker, if play is at, say, 25 yards, is credited with a 35-yard field goal.

The final way of scoring is the safety when two points are credited to the defense if the offensive team is caught in possession in their own end zone.
Summarizing the scoring:

6 pts – touchdown
3 pts – field goal
2 pts – safety
1 pt – conversion

Duration of a game

Playing time consists of one hour, divided into four quarters of fifteen minutes each. There is a fifteen-minute interval between the two halves. It must also be mentioned that when the ball is not in play, the clock is always stopped. It is also stopped when a foul has been committed or a fair catch has been caught. The clock is also stopped when a time out is called. Both teams are allowed three time outs, lasting a maximum two minutes each, during each half. The game, and the clock, are stopped two minutes from the end of each half when the referee calls a time out to allow both teams to plan their final strategies. It is easy to see therefore, in reality, that a game can take anything from two to three hours to complete.

If the scores are level at the completion of the fourth quarter, overtime will be played to try and determine the winner. In the regular NFL season there is only one overtime period and if the scores are still level the game is declared a draw. In a play-off or championship game however, as many periods as needed to obtain a result are played. In both instances the first team to score are the winners.

Starting a game

The referee tosses a coin before the start of a game; the visiting captain has the honour of calling. The winning captain can elect

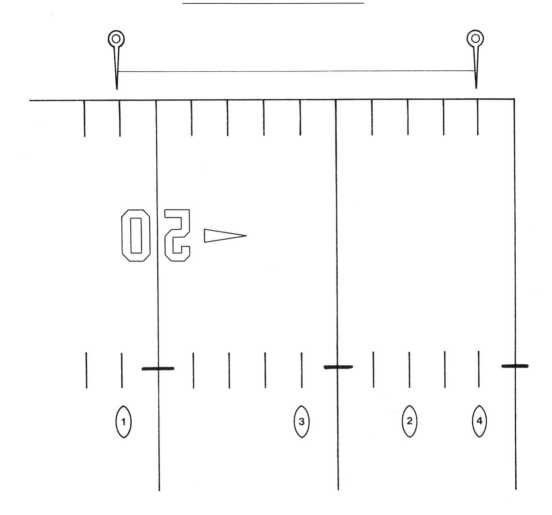

whether his team will be the defense (take the kick) or the offense (receive the kick). When play resumes at the start of the second half the captain who lost the toss at the start of the game has the right to choose. If a game goes into overtime, the captains toss a coin again. In such a situation, as the first team to score wins the game, the captain winning the toss will choose to go on the offense.

Teams change ends at the commencement of each new quarter.

Play is started with a kick-off at the start of the second half, but when the teams turn

Gaining yards

The play commences on the 21-yard line. At the start of play the offense is '1st and 10'. They make 8 yards on the second play (2) and are then '2nd and 2'. On their third play they lose 3 yards, so, with one down left they still have 5 yards to go and are '3rd and 5'. They make the 5 yards and thus complete 10 yards in four downs and have another four downs starting on the 11-yard line.

around at the end of the 1st and 3rd quarters play recommences from the same position of the field (but in the opposite half) where it was halted at the end of that quarter, and the same team retains possession.

The kick-off restarts play after each successful 'point after' attempt, and after each successful field goal attempt. All kick-offs take place on the 35-yard line unless a penalty has been committed. The team making the 'point after' always re-starts the game with the kick-off. If the kick is unsuccessful then the defense starts play from their own 25-yard line and thus becomes the offense.

Object

Once play has started, the object of the offense is to advance up the field and try to score points. The defense try to prevent such a move and in doing so also try to become the offense so they can score points themselves.

To score points the offense must keep possession of the ball. In order to retain possession they must move the ball at least 10 yards forward. They are allowed four attempts (downs) to make the requisite 10 yards. Provided they retain possession while making the 10 yards they then attempt to advance a further 10, again being allowed four downs.

After each attempt at the down the officials measure the distance, and the number of yards gained (or lost) are indicated. The ball is placed on the spot where play is to be re-started from. All plays start in the centre of the field between the hashmarks.

If a team fails to make its 10 yards within four downs then the ball has to be handed over to the opposing team. If a team has little chance of making the 10 yards and only has one down left the ball will generally be punted deep into the defense's part of the field, thus pushing them back into their own territory. At that point the defense become

Re-starting play

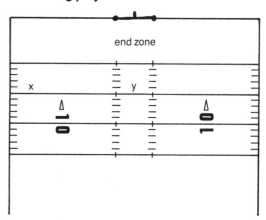

If play ends at point 'x', it is re-started in between the centre lines (inbound lines) at position 'y'.

the offense, and vice versa.

If the offense is caught in possession of the ball behind the line of scrimmage on, say, the first down, then they have to make up those yards lost as well as the 10 yards in their remaining three downs.

Gaining yardage

Moving the ball upfield 10 yards is achieved by a series of 'plays' which are relayed from the coach to the quarterback who is effectively the team leader. Plays are much practised manoeuvres by the offense. Defensive teams will also be aware of their opponents' strategies and thus attempt to foil an effective offense play.

The easiest way to gain yardage is by throwing the ball through the air to a receiver. If successful, a lot of ground can be made. When caught by the receiver it is called a 'completion' but it must be caught clean and the receiver must be in bounds and with both feet on the ground.

Another way of making ground quickly is by the quarterback feeding either his half back or running back who will try and make as much ground as possible by running.

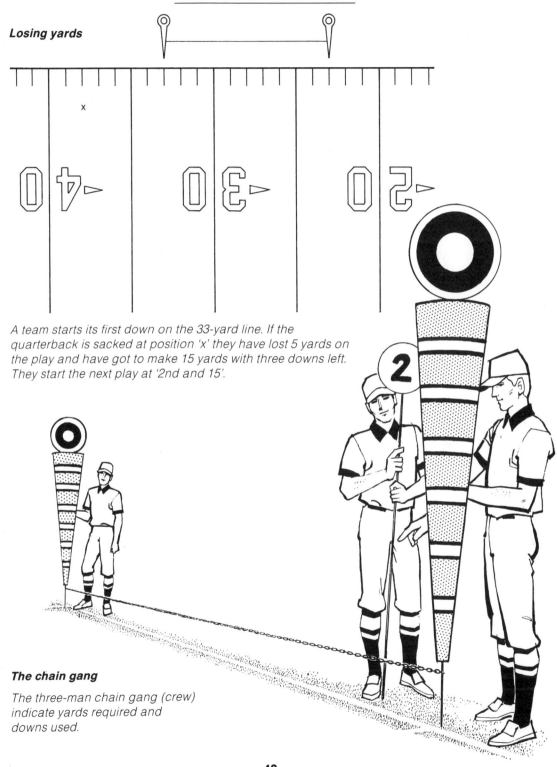

Losing yards

A team starts its first down on the 33-yard line. If the quarterback is sacked at position 'x' they have lost 5 yards on the play and have got to make 15 yards with three downs left. They start the next play at '2nd and 15'.

The chain gang

The three-man chain gang (crew) indicate yards required and downs used.

This is, naturally, called the running game.

The running game can be effective by either running into the defensive pocket, which is usually done in the short yardage situation, or by what is commonly known as the sweep.

The running game is particularly effective when the offense is on or near the opponent's line. A look at the NFL scoring lists will show that running backs regularly top the touchdown scoring charts. It is not just the running backs who have a monopoly on the running game, the quarterback himself may, in extreme circumstances, find no option open to him but to run the ball himself. Set plays like that are rare, but do tend to confuse the defense, and again are more often used in short yardage situations.

WHO · DOES · WHAT?

In soccer the heroes are the players who score the goals; in cricket it is the batsmen who score centuries; and in American football it is the players who make and score the touchdowns who get the glory bestowed upon them. Therefore, it is the quarterback and his receivers who attract the limelight and become household names.

The offense

The front line of the offense is the 'heavy' mob whose duty it is to protect their quarterback from the opposing front line players. The whole operation of the offense is masterminded by the quarterback and he is aided in the quest for points by his running backs and receivers, the men who run upfield and try to catch a pass from the quarterback.

In the offensive line-up, the only players allowed to receive a forward pass are the two players on the extreme end of the line of scrimmage, and any other player situated at

least one yard behind the line of scrimmage. Interior linemen are never allowed to catch a forward pass.

Here is the offensive line-up, with each player's specific role:

Center   An important player on the offense. He is positioned in the middle of the line of scrimmage and it is his job to snap the ball back cleanly to his quarterback. As soon as he makes the snap he is going to be 'steamrollered' by an opposing lineman so he has to be on his guard and ready to block.

Guards   There are two guards, a right guard and a left guard, and they are positioned one either side of the center. Their role is to protect their own ball carrier and prevent any defensive action, by blocking.

Tackles   These guys are pretty tough! There are two tackles, one either side of the guards, and their sole duty is to stop the defense from getting through their lines.

Ends   There are two ends on the offensive line – a right end and a left end. An end positioned right next to a tackle is a tight end and one that is positioned away from the tackle is a split end. Ends are eligible to become ball receivers or can be used as ball carriers, depending on the type of play attempted.

Half back   (Also known as a flanker.) Either one or two half backs will be used, depending upon the type of play. They are quick-running players and are involved in running plays. They are also pass receivers.

Running backs   Again one or two will be used depending upon the type of play. The running back usually lines up behind all the other offensive players and he is used mainly in running plays. Very quick, he should be able to run at, or around, the defense.

Quarterback Finally, the 'brains' of the offense. He is positioned immediately behind the center. He advises the team in the huddle what play they are going to make and he must be quick-thinking and ready to change his plans at the last minute.

The defense

The players who try to prevent the scoring actions are the defensive units, a mean bunch of characters whose main object is to stop the offensive drive and generally to make the quarterback's life sheer misery.

Defensive units are a very close knit clan. Many teams in the NFL have nicknames for their squads. For example, 'The Sack Exchange' form the New York Jets' unit.

The principal objects of the defense are to stop the offense from making yardage and from scoring. This is done basically by tackling and breaking up offensive plays. The defensive team has three regular positions; linemen, linebackers and the secondary.

The aim of the **linemen**, who are positioned on the line of scrimmage, is to rush and try and sack the quarterback, and to stop the offensive ball carrier breaking through the defensive line. The number of linemen depends on the call given by the coach in anticipation of an offensive play.

Linebackers, as their name suggests, take their place directly behind the linemen, occasionally moving to the line of scrimmage to assist the linemen when the offense is on a short yardage situation and a running play is expected. The task of the linebackers is to defend against all plays called by the offense i.e. passing, rushing, or any inventive play from the opposing quarterback. If you do manage to get past the linebackers you are sure to make good ground.

Another part of the defensive team is the **secondary**. They are known as the defensive backs and usually total three or four in number, and are made up of cornerbacks

and safeties. The **cornerbacks'** main functions are to protect the outside flanks against a running play and also cover the wide receivers on passing attempts. Many coaches think that this position is the hardest to play on the defensive unit because a wide receiver receiving a pass from a quarterback will be moving forward and the cornerback has to keep his eye on the runner as well as on the play.

The **safeties** are the last line of defense and are situated deep in the middle of the defensive area. Their priority is to move around the secondary and to give support wherever it is needed most. If an offense lines up with a tight end the safety who is positioned on the same side of the field is the strong safety. The other safety is known as the free safety and has no single task in marking any particular receiver who comes deep.

Those who enjoy the 'hit' and 'be hit' aspect of American football would be right in assuming that defensive players really do enjoy their work. With the exception of facemasking, practically anything goes in sending ball carriers on to the ground. The achievement of that, to a defensive player, is his greatest delight and satisfaction.

Special teams

The special teams are units for performing specific functions. They are used mainly for either kicking or punting, or in the return of both.

Kick-off team   When kicking-off, the kicker has a defensive team with him. A good kicker will try to give the ball height and placement. He will give it height because the longer the ball stays in the air, the more time his team has to move downfield to tackle the receiver – hopefully as close to his own line as possible.

From the kick-off the ball must be kept within the confines of the playing area and a good kicker will try to get the ball to hit the ground and roll, thus making it extremely difficult for the receiver to collect it and enable his own team to make ground. The alternative to the standard kick-off is the onside kick, where a losing team, wanting to

try and keep possession of the ball, kick it along the ground a minimum of 10yd (9·14m) hoping that an awkward rolling ball will be recovered by themselves instead of the opposing receivers, thus giving them the chance of gaining immediate possession.

At all kick-offs the players of the kicking team must be behind the ball at the time of the kick and all receiving team players must be at least 10yd (9·14m) from the ball when the kick is made.

Kick-off return team   The receiving side's mission is to try to protect the receiver, assuming he has made a good catch, and to try to block tacklers, thus enabling their receiver to gain as much yardage as possible. If the protection is good the receiver could possibly run for a touchdown. If the receiver, on catching the ball, feels that he can make no ground, he can call for a fair catch and the offensive drive would start at the point of the catch.

Punting team   The special punting team has more or less the same duties as the kick-off unit. The only difference being that on a kick-off, the ball is kicked from the ground, whereas a punt is kicked after dropping the ball from the hands. The punt is used normally when a team has had three downs and have little chance to make

American Football is one of the most physical of all sports!

their 10 yards and are out of field goal range. The punt will get them out of immediate trouble and after giving possession to the opposing team will see them starting their offensive drive deep in their own half.

To make a punt, the punter lines up about 10yd (9·14m) behind the line of scrimmage and is protected by his linemen, who, after the kicker receives the ball from the snap, will endeavour to keep the punt return unit from harassing him. Like the kick-off team the punt team are also responsible for stopping the receiver from gaining yardage.

Punt return team Like their kick-off return counterparts, the punt return team are responsible for protecting their receiver or ball carrier. In addition they are allowed to try to prevent the opposing punter from making the kick, and to hold their place on the scrimmage line to ensure that a punt does take place and that the opposition has not devised a sneaky run or pass play.

Field goal units The field goal units come into operation when the goal posts are within the range of the offensive team's kicker, and the team is facing a fourth down or, in an overtime situation, feel confident of making the kick with, say, only one down against them, in order to secure the match-winning points.

The kicker and his holder, who more often than not is his quarterback, are again protected by their offensive linemen. After receiving the snap the holder positions the ball on the ground for the kicker to attempt to send it over the crossbar for three points. The defensive unit again has the same priorities as the punt return unit to try to block the kick, prevent the kicker from making the kick and safeguard against the quarterback making a running or passing play instead of going ahead with the kick. Because field goal attempts are made from directly in front of the posts, kickers have a high success rate.

The forward pass

Unlike rugby, the forward pass is allowed, and is very much part of American football. There are, however, limitations to its use.

Any player on the offensive team may throw a forward pass but;

(a) The pass must come from a scrimmage play
(b) Only one forward pass per scrimmage is allowed
(c) The pass must be made from behind the line of scrimmage.

The majority of passes are made by the quarterback, who throws the ball with a spinning action to aid its aerodynamicity. (See the diagram opposite.)

Penalties

There are many ways in which the laws can be infringed and the punishment varies according to the nature of the offence. All infringements are penalized with a loss of yards and in some cases loss of yards and the down. The following is a guide to the main offences and their penalty values:

15 YARDS AND AUTOMATIC FIRST DOWN
– Piling on
– Roughing the passer
– Roughing the kicker

15 YARDS
– Spearing an opponent
– Clipping
– Kicking, batting or pushing a ball that has run loose
– Blocking below the waist
– Unsportsmanlike conduct and uncalled-for rough play

10 YARDS
– Illegally using hands on the offense
– Having an ineligible player upfield for a pass play
– Tripping

Pass

A quarterback gets in a pass before he is sacked. Note how the ball is thrown – pointed end first, and with a twist of the wrist which causes the ball to spin in flight as aerodynamically as possible.

5 YARDS AND AUTOMATIC FIRST DOWN
- Holding by a defender
- Running into the kicker
- Illegally using hands when on the defense

5 YARDS AND LOSS OF DOWN
- Making a forward pass from beyond the line of scrimmage
- Intentional grounding

5 YARDS
- Player out of bounds at the snap
- Forward pass NOT from a scrimmage
- Crawling
- Encroachment
- Kick-off out of bounds

- Accidentally grabbing opponent's facemask
- Any formation, return of punt, shift, substitution or motion that is illegal
- Invalid fair catch signal
- Having less than seven players on the offensive line at the time of the snap
- More than one man in motion at the time of the snap
- Time out in excess of two minutes

LOSS OF DOWN
- A second forward pass from behind the line of scrimmage
- A forward pass which touches an ineligible receiver.

RULES CLINIC

Can any player in the team receive a pass?

No. The offensive linemen, the center, the guards and the tackles are ineligible receivers.

Do both teams have more than one captain?

Yes, they have captains for each of the special units that are on the field at any one time.

After what situations and from where do kick-offs take place?

At the beginning of each half, after each 'point after' attempt, and after a field goal attempt. All kick-offs are taken from the kicking team's 35-yard line, NB: the kicker may at his discretion place the ball in a tee, have another player hold it, or most unlikely, attempt to drop kick it himself.

What is happening when you see all the players gathered round in a huddle before each new play?

The quarterback is giving instructions about the next play to his team mates. These are in accordance with the coach's wishes, which are relayed to the quarterback.

In that case, why does the quarterback occasionally shout at the players immediately prior to the snap taking place?

He is not shouting at the players, he is merely shouting a numerical code, to let his team know there is a change of play, possibly because he has seen an unexpected alteration in the opposition defense.

How long is a team in a huddle allowed to discuss their forthcoming tactics?

They are allowed thirty seconds to bring the ball into play, and if they exceed that limit they are penalized 5 yards. There is an electronic clock in each stadium which is used specifically for the purpose of assisting both players and referee.

How many players of the offensive team must be on the line of scrimmage when the snap is delivered?

At least seven. The other players, except the player who receives the snap, must be at least a yard behind.

RULES · CLINIC

If a team has utilized its four downs and not achieved the necessary 10 yards what happens?

Their opponents take control of the ball at a parallel spot between the centre lines from where the last play came to a halt.

If after three downs a team is on the opposition 25-yard line and decide to go for a field goal, is the kick taken from the 25-yard line?

No. The line of scrimmage would be on that particular line, so the kicker would move back about ten yards and try for a 35-yard field goal.

I understand that only one forward pass is allowed in any one play, but what about laterals, how many of them can be thrown per play?

As many as a team wishes.

How many substitutes may be used in a game?

As many as a team likes. A player can be on the field for one play, off for the next and then back again for the third. Players can be utilized at any time providing only eleven players are on the pitch at any one time.

At a kick-off can the ball be kicked directly into touch?

It can be, but it would cost your team a 5-yard penalty and the kick would have to be retaken from your own 30-yard line.

Why is it advantageous for the quarterback to make the ball spin when he is attempting a pass play?

Because it causes the ball to spiral or rotate which gives it great wind resistance thus giving greater accuracy to the pass.

What is clipping?

A dangerous form of blocking when a player blocks another from behind. Officials keep a careful watch for this offence.

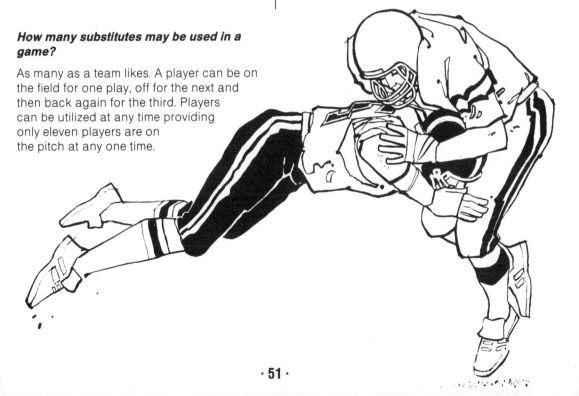

Can I block or interfere with a player attempting to catch a pass?

No. It is illegal to prevent a player making a catch, other than by intercepting it. Accidental interference is not an offence but the official has a difficult task in deciding if interference has taken place and whether it is accidental or not.

Can a player who anticipates making a fair catch make a 'half-hearted' signal, thus giving himself two options after making the catch?

No. If his fair catch signal is not clear he will be penalized 5 yards.

Can a receiver take a pass on the field and then step out of bounds?

Yes, providing both feet were on the ground and within the field of play at the time of making the catch. The next play would then start from a point level with where he went out of bounds.

Can a pass receiver be blocked or baulked on his run downfield?

Once he has gone five yards downfield he is not allowed to be interfered with.

You often see players running along the back of the line of scrimmage, is this permissible?

Yes, otherwise you wouldn't see it . . . however, it is not players but a player, as only one member of the offensive team in the backfield is allowed to move prior to the snap and then he is allowed only to move parallel to or away from the line of scrimmage. It is an illegal motion otherwise.

Can I help the ball carrier by, say, trying to push him over the line?

No, helping the ball carrier is an offence.

Can an ineligible receiver move downfield?

Only after the ball has been passed. If he moves downfield before then it is a penalty.

If a punt goes out of bounds where does play start from?

If it goes over the sidelines play starts in the middle sector of the field at a point level to where it left the field. If the punt goes into the opposing end zone then the opposing team start their 1st and 10 from their own 20-yard line.

For a touchdown, can a player dive rugby-style and put the ball into the end zone even though his body may not be entirely in the end zone?

Yes, that is perfectly OK.

If a pass is incomplete, can an opposing player collect the ball and gain possession?

No. After an incompletion your side retains possession but the ball is returned to the point where the last play started from, and you have one less down to go.

William Perry of the Chicago Bears – otherwise known as 'The Refrigerator', due to his solid build!

What happens if there are infringements at the 'point after' attempt?

If the infringement is by the defensive team then they are penalized. If, say, it is a 5-yard penalty, then when the kick-off is taken the kick will be from the kicking team's 40-yard line and not their 35-yard line, If the infringement is by the offensive team then the 'point after' kick has to be taken again, but 5yd (4·57m) further away from the goal.

How do the chain crew indicate yardage?

One member of the crew holds his marker level with the point of the start of the first play and the other will stand along the touchline ten yards away (the length of the chain between the two poles). They will not move until the 10 yards have been gained. The third member of the crew holds an indicator stating which down is next and he will stand at a point level with where the last down was made.

What does 1st and 10, 2nd and 7 . . . and so on mean?

It indicates how many yards the offensive side still has to make, and the number of downs used. 1st and 10 means the play is the first down with the full 10 yards still to be made, 2nd and 7 means the next play is the second down and the offense still has to make 7 yards.

What happens if the receiver and a defender catch the ball simultaneously?

The pass is deemed to be complete and the receiver keeps possession.

TECHNIQUE

American football's principal techniques fall into two distinct categories, those of the offense and those of the defense. But within those two basic elements of the game there is much more to concentrate on. Offensive players need to be good blockers, ball handlers, runners, and receivers. Defensive players need to be good rushers and tacklers. But that is not all; there are also the field goal experts, the punters, and then there are the men who catch and return field goal and punt attempts. All are specific roles on the field of play, and all are approached differently. You can't just run on a field and say 'I'm a footballer' . . . you're not just that. You are either a quarterback, a running back, a guard, a tackle, a punter, or whatever. Each player has a specific role.

As the game revolves around a series of plays, i.e. the offensive manoeuvre to advance the ball 10 yards within four downs, we ought to start at the obvious starting place, and look at what a play is.

All plays are called by the coach, who relays it to his quarterback who, in turn, relays it to his team-mates. Your coach could set up the best play in the world, but without knowing how the defense will react to it, the end product is an unknown quantity . . . if that wasn't the case, boy, would it be a boring sport! For that reason, it is pointless to go into lengthy details about plays; after all, it is the 'ifs and buts' that decide the outcome, and believe me, there are plenty of those in American football!

Right, let's have a look at an offensive play for starters, and get right among the thick of the action:

THE · OFFENSE

The idea of all offensive plays is for the linemen to fend off the marauding defenders by blocking, so as to create room for a player to either run downfield and collect a pass from his quarterback (a passing play), or to create an opening for one of the running backs to run through (a running play).

In this close yardage situation, there are only 6yd (5·48m) to the goal line. Both sides are packing the line of scrimmage tightly

A short yardage play

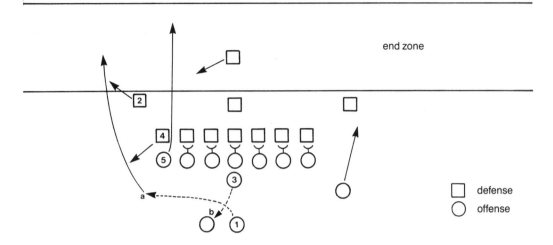

Running back ① *is the key to this play. His initial run before the snap puts defenders* ② *and* ④ *'on guard'. As* ① *makes his run after the snap,* ④ *goes after him, thus creating the 'hole' for tight end* ⑤ *to get through and reach the end zone for a touchdown.*

and the chance of a running play is remote. The best play would be for one of the ends to break through the line of defense and get into the end zone ready to take a pass.

Before the snap, running back ① runs to position a, this would cause cornerback ② to move to his right to provide cover ready for the break. At the snap the quarterback ③ takes the ball and steps back to position b. As the linemen get on with their blocking the defensive end ④ moves to his right in an effort to block the running back. This will then leave a gap for the tight end ⑤ to make a run into the end zone. All that is left to do is for the quarterback to make a successful throw to his receiver.

There are many plays, standard, or a variety of a standard play. They number too many to show you. While all are different, the principle is the same in all, to create room for the quarterback to throw the ball and for runners to get through the defensive line, either with the ball or to take a thrown pass. The defense, on the other hand, try and prevent such action by rushing the opposition and by tackling the ball carrier.

Passing play

One way the offense can get the ball downfield is by a passing play, utilizing the forward pass. The quarterback, after stepping back and surveying the position of his receiver(s), will make the pass, and hopefully the catch will be made, and yards will be gained.

All this sounds easy but it is far from that. Although the move will have been worked out and well practised in advance, it is a different matter when it comes down to the realities of life. The difficult job for the

At scrimmage line: the quarterback waits to receive the 'snap' from his center.

Play action

The commonly used play action, involving the quarterback and one of his backs. It is an effective fake which often confuses the opposing defense.

receiver is getting away from the defensive player and he does this by a series of jinks and dummies around the field until he arrives at a position where his quarterback is expecting him to be.

Another form of a passing play is the **play action**, but this time without the aid of the forward pass. It is an effective play involving the quarterback and his running back and has confused many a defense over the years.

The quarterback turns, as if he is making a pass to the running back. The running back then fakes and pretends to take the ball, and runs downfield. The defense, thinking he has the ball, make him their target, only to see the quarterback run off with the ball, and around his linemen.

Defensive players, however, are not as dumb as I'm painting them. They are aware of play actions and often prevent them, but they still need that split second to decide whether it was fake pass or not. That split second can often mean the difference between a successful and an unsuccessful play.

The **screen pass** is an offensive play that lulls the defense into a false sense of security. The linemen allow the defense to break through their lines and the quarterback, who has stepped well back, will pump his arm a couple of times as if he were going to make a long throw downfield.

The first action of allowing the defense through gives the offensive ends or running backs the chance to advance downfield. The action of faking a long throw keeps the defensive backs downfield but the quarterback then makes a throw to a receiver who has run into a position just ten to fifteen yards away. Mind you, the quarterback has to be quick-witted . . . once those defensive linemen have broken through there is more chance of stopping a steamroller!

The offense has an alternative to the passing play, and that is the running play. Let us look at some examples:

TECHNIQUE

Screen pass

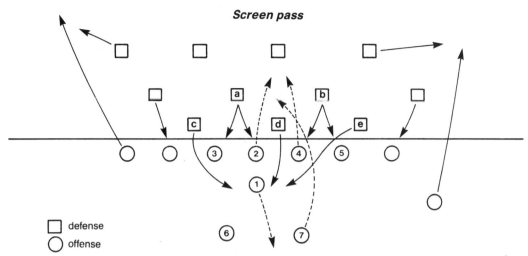

Quarterback ① drops back, defenders [c], [d] and [e] are allowed to break through the ranks. There are only two linebackers, [a] and [b] to then take care of the centre ②, guards ③ and ④ and right tackle ⑤. The odds are now in the offense's favour. Let's say ② and ④ are left alone by the linebackers. They will move downfield and act as blockers for back ⑦, who moves behind them and then takes the short pass from his quarterback.

The draw play

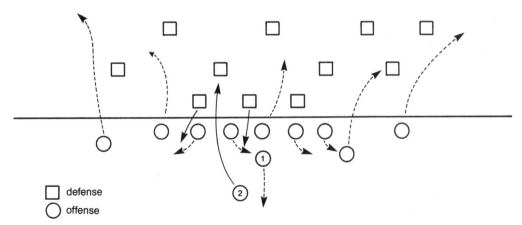

The offensive line-up seems to be for a passing play, and indeed the movement of all players gives that impression. But once the left guard and left tackle have created the 'hole', the quarterback will hand-off to his running back ②, who will set off on a run.

The quarterback sneak

From the snap the quarterback, protected by his defender, makes a charge.

Running plays

An effective running play is the **sweep**, whereby the ball carrier is protected by two blockers and goes wide around his linemen. When the blockers have done their job, the back carries on running and into an open space which his blockers will, hopefully, have created.

If successful, the **trap** is one of the most spectacular running plays. It is another one of the many fakes within the sport. This time, one of the middle linemen, center, tackle or guard, rather than hold his ground and make the block, moves away to one side (this is eventually going to be the 'hole' the running back will come through). The defensive lineman then goes to fill the gap but another offensive lineman comes round the back and blocks *him* thus creating the gap for the running back.

Another fake play is the **draw play**. In this play the offensive formation gives the impression it is for a passing play . . . but that is only to fool the opposition; it is really a running play. Every player assumes positions for the passing play, even the receivers run in standard passing patterns. The quarterback also steps back as if to make a pass but, when the 'hole' has been created in the defense he will hand-off the ball to his running back who will make for the gap.

On short yardage plays the **quarterback sneak** is often employed. This play creates a gap in the defense, through which the quarterback himself can run.

Another short yardage play is the **bootleg**. As the two sets of linemen are grouped together at the line of scrimmage there is a chance of a quick play by the offense around the tight ends . . . but the defense will be wary of this. To carry out the bootleg, the quarterback fakes a hand-off to his running back who makes for the middle of the scrimmage, thus attracting the attention of the defenders, and sneakily, the quarterback will make the run himself around the outside of his linemen, highlighting once again just how versatile he must be.

Bootleg

At the snap, running back ① makes a run for the middle of the line and quarterback ② fakes a hand-off. He keeps the ball and heads quickly towards the touchdown. Ideal in close yardage situations.

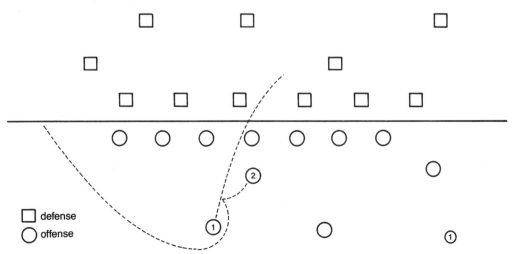

defense
offense

This is how offensive linemen stand at the scrimmage.

Standard offensive line formations

Some standard offensive line formations, and when they are likely to be used:

The **pro set**. The standard offensive line-up is the pro set formation with one tight end, one split end, a wide receiver and two running backs . . . in addition to the quarterback and five middle-linemen.

The **I formation** is an ideal formation for running plays. The 'I' formed behind the center gives the running back plenty of time to assess the situation in front of him and wait for the 'hole' to appear in the defense before he sets off on his run.

The **T formation** is used for a running play normally where the quarterback will hand-off to one of his running backs who will attempt to go around the outside of the linemen.

The **shotgun** is a popular formation in the passing game. The quarterback takes the snap well behind the line of scrimmage (five to seven yards) and by the time he is ready to make the forward pass he will have, hopefully, his five receivers downfield.

The **short yardage formation** is employed when there are only a couple of yards to go to the goal line or for the first down.

Pass patterns

Receivers run to set pass patterns. The part of the field they run to is all part of the well-rehearsed 'plan' before each play. It is, of course, the defense's job to prevent him reaching his destination.

The run will normally be pre-determined but, obviously, the runner has to exercise his right to choose where to go if the original

The quarterback (no 16) gets the play moving from the 'snap'.
Note the protection he receives from his linemen.

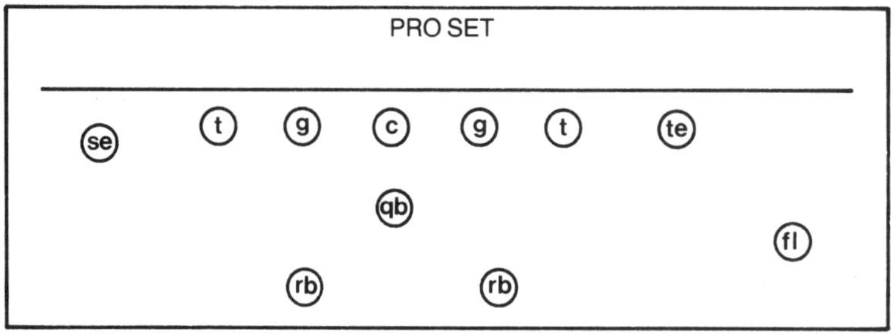

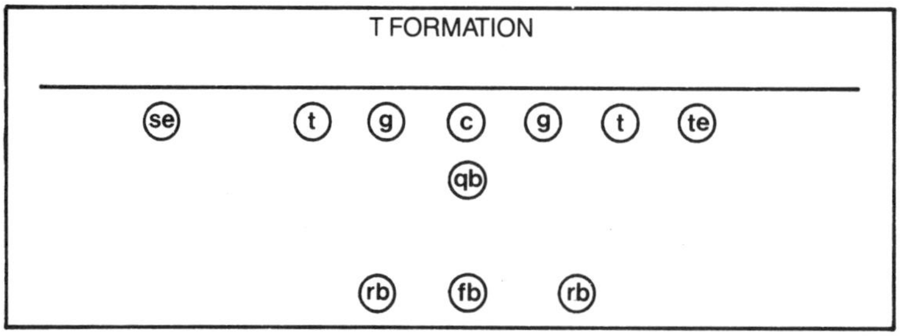

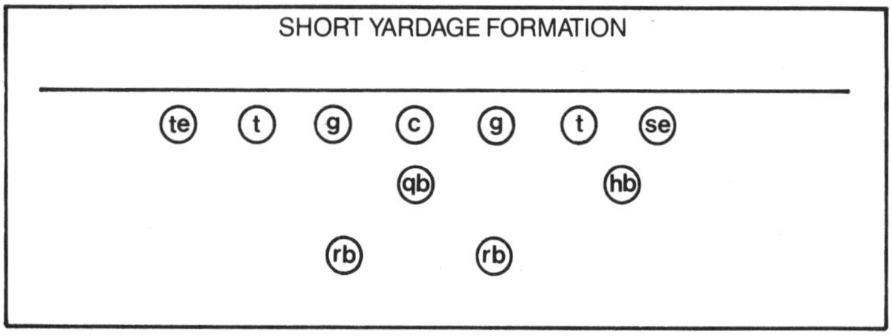

PRO SET

se · t · g · c · g · t · te
qb
fl
rb · rb

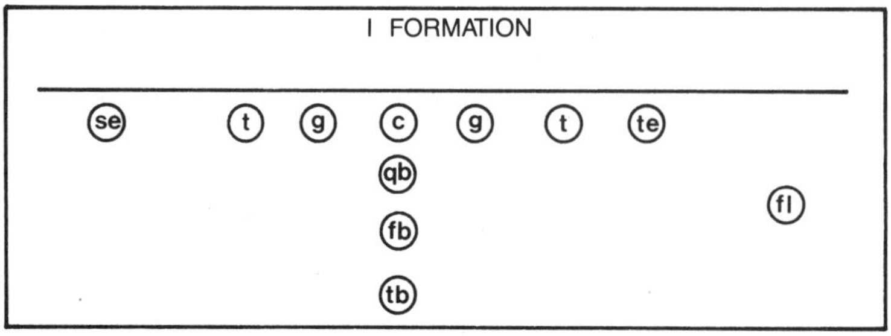

I FORMATION

se · t · g · c · g · t · te
qb
fb
tb
fl

T FORMATION

se · t · g · c · g · t · te
qb
rb · fb · rb

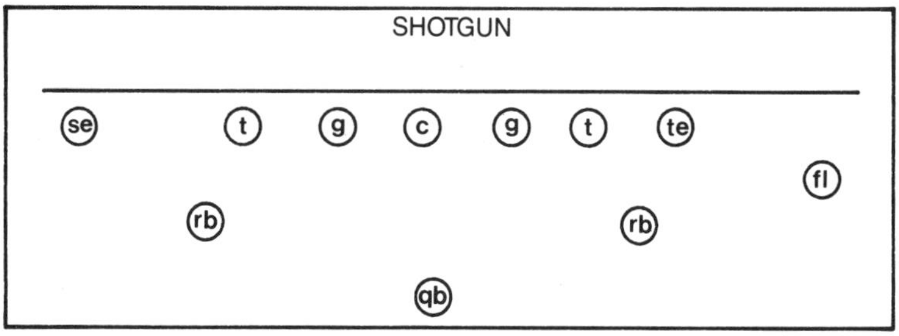

SHOTGUN

se · t · g · c · g · t · te
rb · rb
fl
qb

SHORT YARDAGE FORMATION

te · t · g · c · g · t · se
qb · hb
rb · rb

Offensive formations

qb quarterback
c   center
se split end
te tight end
g   guard
t   tackle
rb running back
fl flanker/wide
    receiver
fb full back
tb tail back
hb half back

TECHNIQUE

Passing patterns *Passing patterns for a wide receiver.*

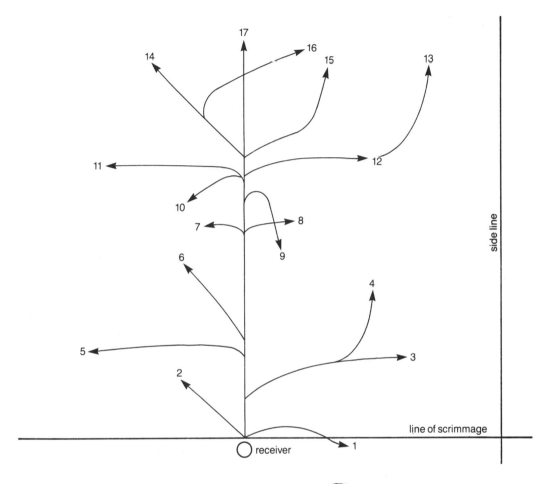

17
16
15
14
13
11
12
10
7 8
9
6
4
5
3
2
side line
line of scrimmage
◯ receiver
1

1 screen
2 slant
3 short out
4 short out and up
5 cross
6 quick post
7 hook in
8 hook out
9 comeback
10 curl
11 in
12 out
13 out and fly
14 post
15 fly
16 corner
17 up

AMERICAN · FOOTBALL

Passing patterns for a tight end.

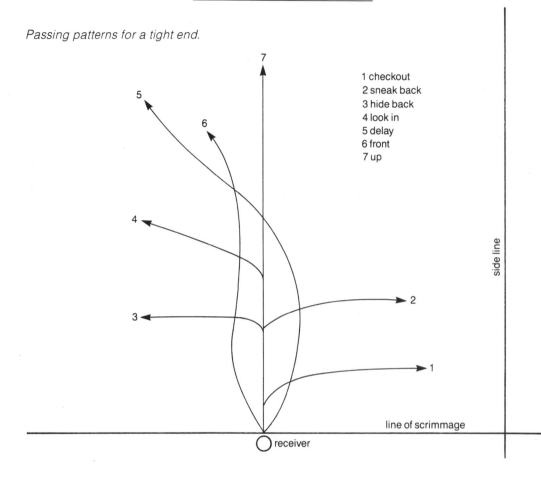

1 checkout
2 sneak back
3 hide back
4 look in
5 delay
6 front
7 up

side line

line of scrimmage

receiver

destination is not a wise idea. This is when it calls for an alert quarterback to see any shift in movement of his receiver. Most teams work to a basic set of pass patterns and those shown are the generally recognized names given to them. Teams, however, call them by other names. . . . If they don't come off, I'm sure they are suitably re-named with an appropriate expletive!

TECHNIQUE

Passing patterns for the running backs.

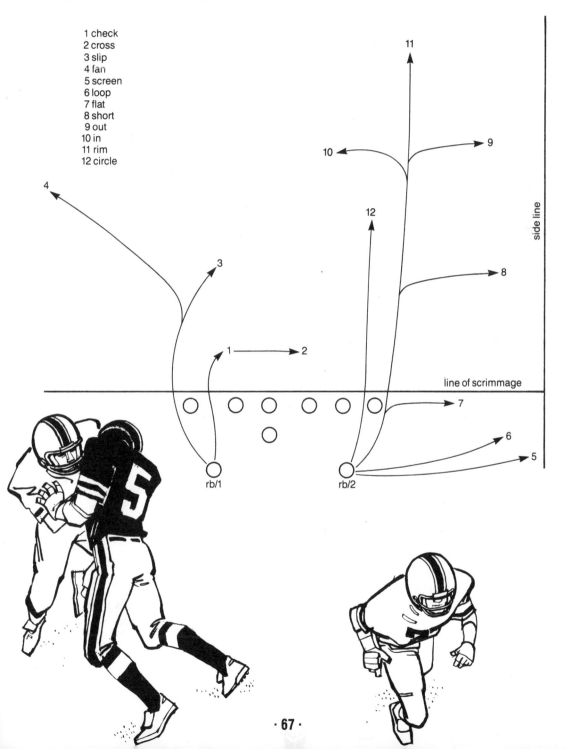

1 check
2 cross
3 slip
4 fan
5 screen
6 loop
7 flat
8 short
9 out
10 in
11 rim
12 circle

side line

line of scrimmage

rb/1

rb/2

THE · DEFENSE

The defense's job is to stop the offense making its 10 yards and to stop them from scoring. To do this they can either tackle, or break up any offensive play by rushing the offense. But the defender's lot is not an easy one. The linemen have to contend with the offensive blockers; the safeties and cornerbacks have to follow receivers as they wander around the park ready to get into a good receiving position; and of course there is still the tackling to be done . . .

To make a successful **tackle** the ball carrier must be pulled, pushed, grabbed, or knocked to the ground by a defender, and be unable to move any further forward. Runners who are likely to be tackled often run with their knees high, thus making the tackle more difficult. Tackling is not easy because the runner has the freedom to use any part of the ball park he chooses. He therefore holds the initiative.

Defensive plays

There are many different defensive plays and one of the most spectacular is the **blitz**, which is the defense's attempt to sack the quarterback. The secondary, either on their own or accompanied by the linebackers, will rush through the scrimmage line in an attempt to get at the quarterback. However, a quarterback seeing such a move might often call an audible and make a pass just over the line of scrimmage. However . . . and the plot thickens, the defense may fake a blitz in order to get the quarterback to call an audible, and hopefully get possession from the offensive side . . . this game gets more like 'Call My Bluff' all the time!

Another defensive play is the **Slant**. On the call, the defensive linemen charge to either the right or left instead of straight on. **Stack** play poses a problem to the offensive linemen who do not know where the linebacker is going to charge. He lines up immediately behind one of his linemen, and

The blitz

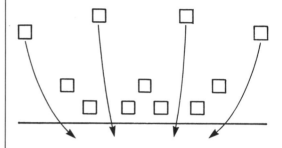

This is the defensive formation for the blitz. On the snap, the secondary rush forward in an attempt to sack the quarterback.

The slant

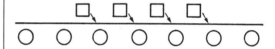

At the snap, the four defensive linemen charge at an angle rather than straight ahead. This gives the opportunity of, in this case, the linebackers and secondary on the far left to 'attack' the offense.

The stack

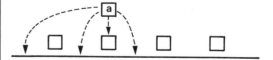

The linebacker takes up a position immediately behind his lineman. The opposition can hardly see him and are uncertain where he will make his first charge from.

TECHNIQUE

Zones

The area behind the front line of defense is divided into imaginary zones, and players are assigned specific zones to defend.

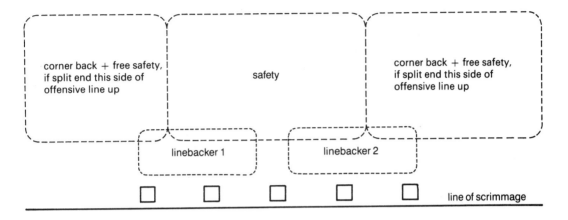

corner back + free safety, if split end this side of offensive line up

safety

corner back + free safety, if split end this side of offensive line up

linebacker 1

linebacker 2

line of scrimmage

Zones are not marked on the pitch, but experience soon tells you which is your 'territory'.

has the chance to charge the opposition to the right, left, or straight on if he wishes.

Zones

Successful defense is not only built around good blocking and tackling, but also with sound coverage of the various parts of their own territory, known as zones. All zones must be covered adequately by a defender otherwise a slick offensive player will soon exploit the situation.

Zone defense is an imaginary group of zones on the field and each player has the specific job of following a receiver who moves into that zone.

Man-to-man covering is not a tactic used all that often in American football, unlike other team contact sports. The offense has the advantage with man-to-man marking and often long passes are completed. The **bump** is a one-to-one marking situation with the defensive back closely marking an eligible receiver. The moment the receiver

sets off on his run the defender is allowed to bump (baulk) him, but it must be within five yards of his setting off. It may not prevent the run, but it will, just for that split second, delay the receiver, or better still – put him off.

So, what about defensive formations and when they are used?

Defensive formations

The **6-5 goal line defense** is used in a short yardage situation. There are six linemen and five linebackers. There isn't likely to be a long pass in a short yardage situation so the short pass, and the run, need watching. The linebackers look out for the short pass and the linemen for the short run.

The **3-4 defense**. With having only three front linemen the four linebackers can, at the snap, either rush the passer or go after the ball carrier if it is a running play.

The **4-3 defense** is quite often used when a pass play is anticipated in the hope that the four front men can prevent the pass.

AMERICAN · FOOTBALL

Defensive formations

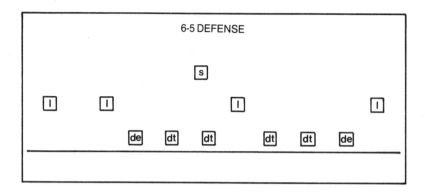

6-5 DEFENSE

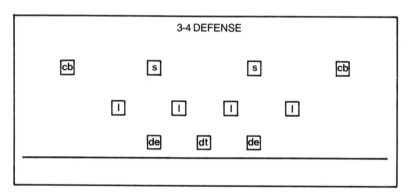

3-4 DEFENSE

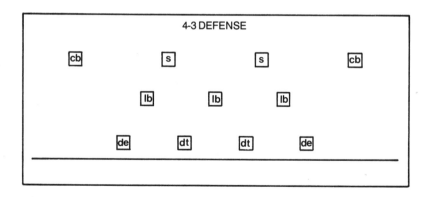

4-3 DEFENSE

dt defensive tackle
de defensive end
l   linebackers
s   safety
cb cornerback

Blocking
A good example of a block

Blocking

Good blocking is the key to successful offense. Blocking can take two forms, either blocking a defender from getting into the offense's backfield, or by acting as a 'guard' for his running back and running in front of him, removing any oncoming defenders in his wake.

Quarterbacks and running backs get all the glory in the offensive unit but the role of the linemen should never be forgotten.

When blocking, the upper part of the body only can be used and his hands must be completely- or half-closed at the time of the block. You are not allowed to interlock your hands, nor interlock arms with another blocker. Tripping, spearing and facemasking are also out of the question, but brute force is allowed . . . it is part of the blockers credentials for getting the job in the first place!

The basic types of block are with the head (but remember, no spearing), the shoulders, the body, and the arms.

Catching

In making all catches the ball must be caught cleanly and the receiver must have control of it. When making a fair catch remember you must signal your intention while the ball is in flight. If you don't you will

This is one way of making sure the ball carrier is well and truly grounded.

be penalized five yards. After taking a fair catch you are allowed to take two steps forward. Any more than two and it is illegal.

Tackling

The only person who can be tackled is the ball carrier. Once the defensive lineman has broken through the offense's block, his next job is to get to the quarterback and try for the sack. It is important to tackle the ball carrier above the waist, that way his momentum will carry him backwards after the tackle and, effectively, lose him yardage.

and finally . . .

The New York Giants' kicker in action.

Kicking

Kicking the field goal. The catcher takes the ball from the snap and holds it on the ground for the kicker.

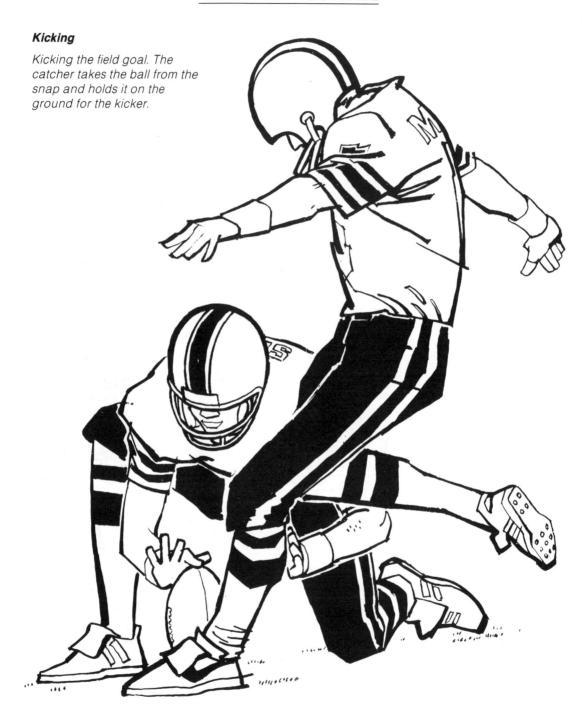

Kicking

American football is not only about the passing and running game, there is also the kicking aspect. Punters and field goal experts are a vital part of the offensive team's artillery, and kick-off and punt return teams are vital parts of the defensive team's set up.

The returner's job after making the catch is to advance upfield as quickly and as far as he can. He does this by a series of sidesteps and deceptive runs. Once he has made ground, and the first down he and his 'team' leave the field and the offensive battery of the team takes over.

Kicking in American football is unlike that in rugby. The ball is not kicked from dead-ball situations, except the kick-off. For all other kicks the ball is snapped back from the scrimmage. In the case of a field goal it is snapped back to a ball handler who holds the ball in position for the kicker. On the punt, it is snapped back directly to the kicker.

At the kick-off however, the ball is either held by a handler, kicked from a kicking tee, or drop-kicked. The punt is kicked by dropping the ball from the kicker's hands and kicking it before it hits the ground.

Punting

The punt:
1. *the kick is lined up.*
2. *the ball is dropped from the kicker's hands.*
3. *the ball is kicked before it touches the ground.*

It is easy to see why American Football creates so much interest in the United States. It is a multi-million dollar sport which culminates in the Superbowl each January. British fans are just as 'hooked' on that great occasion and, as you sit through three or four hours of plays, you will soon appreciate the subtleties which make this sport so intriguing. It is not brute force alone that wins games – a quick-thinking brain also comes in handy!

That's about it . . . that's American football. It sounds complicated with all its passes, rushes, blocks, punts, tackles and so on, but it is not. It is really a simple game. It is a great game to play, a great game to watch. Hopefully, we have given you an insight into the finer points of the game without baffling you with science . . . We'll leave that to the professional coaches.

A New York Jets running back falters during a game against New England.

USEFUL

ADDRESSES

British American Football Association
92 Palace Garden Terrace
London W8 4RS

Budweiser League
30–35 Drury Lane
London
WC2B 5RH

National Football League
(& AFC/NFC)
410 Park Avenue
New York
NY 10022
USA

National Collegiate Athletic Association
US Highway 50
Nall Avenue at 63rd Street
Box 1906
Mission
Kansas 66201
USA

RULES CLINIC
INDEX

INDEX